Foreword

Owning a hamster is great fun but a huge responsibility. All animals need a regular routine and lots of love and attention from us. But most importantly, pets need owners who are going to stay interested in them and committed to them all their lives.

Anyone who has ever enjoyed the company of a pet knows just how strong the bond can be. Children learn the meaning of loyalty, unselfishness and friendship by growing up with animals. Elderly or lonely people often depend on a pet for company and it has been proved that animals can help in the prevention of and recovery from physical or mental illness.

The decision to bring a pet into your home should always be discussed and agreed by everyone in the family. Bear in mind that parents are ultimately responsible for the health and well-being of the animal for the whole of its lifetime. If you are not prepared for the inevitable expense, time, patience and occasional frustration involved, then the RSPCA would much rather that you didn't have a pet.

Being responsible for a pet will completely change your life but if you make the decision to go ahead, think about offering a home to one of the thousands of animals in RSPCA animal centres throughout England and Wales. There are no animals more deserving of loving owners.

As for the care of your pet, this book should provide you with all the information you need to know to keep it happy and healthy for many years to come. Enjoy the experience!

Steve Cheetham MA, VetMB, MRCVS
Chief Veterinary Officer, RSPCA

Introduction

At the beginning of the twentieth century, the Golden Hamster was thought to be extinct. In 1930, however, an exciting discovery was made: a female and her young were found in the Syrian desert. They were taken into captivity for breeding, and they became the ancestors of the huge number of laboratory and pet hamsters which have since been reared throughout the world. Sometimes two entirely different species, the Chinese and Russian Hamsters, are available (see pages 9–10) but, except where otherwise stated, this book is concerned with the Golden or Syrian Hamster.

Keeping hamsters as pets

Hamsters still retain their place among the most popular pet rodents. They have proved themselves attractive, undemanding, clean and easily tamed. Potential owners must also realize that they are solitary animals, largely nocturnal by nature, and extremely active.

Fighting amongst hamsters

The fact that the Syrian Hamster is solitary may be an advantage. It is one of the few pet animals that may properly, indeed must, be kept singly. Those owners who attempt to keep two or more adult hamsters together are subjecting them to unwarranted stress, and inviting conflict that invariably results in injury and death. These animals become gentle and tractable with people but will fight viciously with each other.

In the wild, Golden Hamsters are nocturnal, or perhaps crepuscular (active at dawn and dusk). In captivity, they may adapt sufficiently to wake during the afternoon, but the principal periods of activity remain the night, dawn and dusk. It is at these times – and therefore often unseen – that hamsters will fight among themselves.

Active creatures

Since hamsters are often seen during their daytime rest period, many people make the understandable but quite wrong assumption that they are indolent animals. The reverse is true. Hamsters are highly active during their waking hours, occupying themselves by running on a wheel, climbing, gnawing, grooming, rearranging their bedding and escaping.

▶ The Golden, or Syrian, Hamster is one of the few pet animals that must be housed singly.

Varieties

Syrian (Golden) Hamsters

The natural colour of these hamsters is a rich golden brown above, with a white underside. The face is marked with white crescents beneath dark cheek flashes. Since their introduction to Britain in 1931, Golden Hamsters have been bred so skilfully and extensively that they now occur in over 100 colour varieties.

Self colours

Single-coloured hamsters are known as 'selfs', and the self colours include white, cream, fawn, honey, cinnamon grey, silver blue, sepia, chocolate and various shades of the natural golden colour. Each shade, if recognized by the Hamster Fancy breeders' organization, is referred to as a separate breed, the name of which may include the eye or ear colour, as in the Red-Eyed Cream, Black-Eyed White, Dark-Eared Albino, and Flesh-Eared Albino. Perhaps surprisingly, there are no black hamsters, despite the optimistic claims of enthusiasts. There are many dark-coated hamsters, but on examination they are found to have lighter bellies, frequently a lighter ring around the eyes, and they do not 'breed true'.

▲ Dark Golden Syrian Hamster

▶ Longhaired Red-eyed Cream Syrian

▶ Black-Eyed Cream Syrian

Marked varieties

The marked varieties are the multi-coloured or patterned hamsters. The most commonly seen is the banded variety, which has a broad white band across the hamster's back, dividing the self colour into two sections. Banded hamsters are named according to their self colour, as for example, in the Golden Band, Honey Band and the Ruby-Eyed Fawn Band Hamsters.

Other marked varieties of multi-coloured or patterned hamsters include the Piebald, which is broken-coloured with some white-spotting; the Mosaic, which has one or more dark markings on a pale coat; and the Tortoiseshell and White Hamster, which has three colours, including yellow, in the coat.

▼ Grey Syrian Hamster ▶ Golden Hamster and young

► Longhaired Syrian Hamster

Varying coat-types

Golden Hamsters have been successfully bred with varying coats, which may be both longer and shorter than the natural form. The longhaired varieties have an appealing, fluffy look and they are bred in the whole range of colour varieties. The shorthaired form is the satinized hamster with fur that looks and feels rather like velvet. These, hamsters, too, are bred in the complete range of available colours.

◄ Cinnamon Satin Syrian Hamster

Social hamsters

There has long been a demand from pet keepers for a social hamster which will live peaceably in a colony. Breeders have sought to meet this demand by offering two species of hamster that are known to live in groups in the wild. Both are small animals, less than half the size of the Golden Hamster, and the colour varieties are limited.

Chinese Hamsters

Cricetulus griseus, despite its common name, occurs throughout much of Eurasia from Siberia to Tibet, and westwards into eastern Europe. This species is now available to pet keepers, and they may be kept in pairs of males or females but should be introduced under the age of six weeks. Colony rearing in the close confines of captivity has not always been very successful. Some of the females are highly aggressive and, particularly when they become pregnant, are very liable to attack the males unmercifully, making it imperative to house them separately.

◀ The Chinese Hamster has a long tail and is sometimes known as the Rat-tailed Hamster. Its coat is naturally brown with black ticking and a distinctive dorsal stripe.

Russian Hamsters

Phodopus sungorus occurs throughout Russia, China and Mongolia. These little dwarf hamsters seem to be much more amenable to family life than the Chinese Hamster, and are becoming increasingly popular as pets. Their natural colour is brownish grey with contrasting white underneath and a distinctive black dorsal stripe, but they are now available in a satinized form and also a wide range of coat colours, which include Cinnamon, Chocolate, Opal, Copper and Black.

▲ The Black Campbell's Russian Hamster is a new colour of European origin.

▼ Russian Hamsters are smaller than the Syrian. Three streaks of brownish grey fur often protrude down the side of their bodies into the lighter coloured fur underneath.

▶ A Cinnamon Campbell's Russian Hamster has a prominent dorsal stripe and white underparts.

Hamsters in the Syrian desert

The Golden Hamster is one of those remarkable rodents which is able to survive in the desert where temperatures fluctuate wildly between day and night, vegetation is minimal and rainfall very low. Some dew is formed by the daily variation in temperature, and this is probably the main source of water for desert rodents.

Surviving the sun and heat

In order to survive, hamsters have to avoid the drying effect of the sun and are, therefore, forced to spend almost all of their time in darkness. They have to sleep underground during the day, only venturing out in the evening as the sun goes down.

The hamsters' main defence against daytime heat, and consequent dehydration, is their habit of burrowing. During the day, these animals rest quietly underground where they are well insulated against high surface temperatures by as much as a metre's depth of soil.

Feeding in the desert

In the evening, hamsters become active and they emerge from their own extensive system of tunnels to roam the desert in search of food. Supplies are scant and are thought to consist mainly of dry seeds that are sifted from the desert soil. Sometimes these seeds are supplemented by green food which occasionally becomes available. It is also possible that hamsters may eat some insects.

Temperatures in the desert can fall dramatically at night, but the fur-bearing hamster is insulated against this night-time cold. Hamsters are thought to travel long distances, using their cheek pouches to carry food back to the home burrow where it is hoarded in a separate underground compartment. In this way, hamsters are able to regulate their uncertain food supply; laying in stores in times of relative plenty, and using them in times of shortage.

Solitary animals

As far as we know, hamsters are lone animals. Once they reach adulthood, they live a solitary existence, only seeking out a partner for mating and staying with them briefly. The female tends her young alone, until they are of an age to fend for themselves and to establish their own territories. It is for this reason that hamsters should be kept alone in captivity from the age of about five weeks.

Biology

Colour As reflected in its Latin name, the natural fur colour of *Mesocricetus auratus* is golden (Latin *aurum*, gold), so it is, therefore, correct to refer to these hamsters as 'golden hamsters'. However, many mutations have appeared in captivity and Golden Hamsters now occur in a wide range of colours.

Cheek pouches The presence of cheek pouches is a remarkable adaptation to a desert habitat. All rodents are able to divide their mouth into two by drawing a fold of skin from the cheeks into the gap (the diastema) between the front and the back teeth. In some species, including hamsters, the folds of skin have evolved into permanent cheek pouches which are an important aid to survival. Pouched rodents are able to eke out an existence in arid country, where food supplies are sparse, by ranging over an extensive area and using their cheek pouches to transport food to their underground hoard. The common name 'hamster' is derived from the German verb meaning 'to hoard'. A hamster with its pouches stuffed full of seeds can look puffy around the face, and will have a completely different appearance when it has disgorged its hoard into its larder. The cheek pouches are separate from the mouth and their rather delicate lining is easily lacerated by sharp seeds, straw, thistle-heads, softwoods and such like, all of which should be avoided.

Eyes and eyesight The bright, beady eyes of a healthy hamster are strikingly attractive, but its eyesight is poor. Hamsters are, by nature, burrowing animals. They spend the daylight hours resting underground and emerge only at dusk to forage for food, which they find by sifting the desert soil with their forefeet. Golden Hamsters spend most of their life in darkness, and rely very little on their sense of sight which is poorly developed as a result and rather myopic.

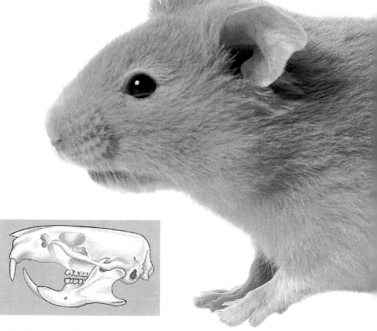

▲ Skull showing long incisors

Teeth The long incisor teeth at the front of the jaw grow continuously, as in all rodents, and must be trimmed. The easiest, most natural way to deal with this is to keep a gnawing block in the hamster's accommodation, together with unshelled brazil nuts and hard food,

Fur People sometimes question why a desert animal, such as the hamster, should be fur-bearing. The explanation is that fur acts as an insulator against heat and cold, and desert animals need protection from both extremes of climate. At night, when hamsters are active, the lack of cloud cover over the desert allows the daytime build-up of heat to escape quickly, causing temperatures to plummet; this means that the days can be very hot and the nights very cold.

such as raw carrot. Neglecting to take these measures may cause the incisors to become overgrown and this will interfere with feeding. A hamster that spends a lot of time gnawing the bars of its metal cage may be lacking more suitable objects for gnawing.

Scent gland The dark spots on each hip (which show particularly on the male) are scent glands. Hamsters spend most of their time in darkness in the wild and are more dependent on their sense of smell than on their sense of sight. The scent glands are used to mark territory, but their more particular use seems to be as an aid to finding a mate, as they dry out once the breeding age is passed.

Agility Despite its remarkably short tail, the hamster's body shape is mouse-like as is its agility. A hamster may spend hours sleeping, or will curl up contentedly in a child's hands but it will also climb curtains, dig furiously, run long distances on an exercise wheel, swing from the bars of a cage, gnaw endlessly and escape from almost anywhere. Hamsters deprived of activity in laboratory conditions have quickly succumbed to a stress-linked disease. It seems they fare best when able to attain a high level of activity. Bear this in mind when you are designing their accommodation.

Hibernation The Golden Hamster is unique because it is the only mammal commonly kept as a pet which also hibernates. Studies have shown that the tendency to hibernate is passed on genetically; breeders have eliminated the trait as far as possible. Even so, some hamsters will hibernate if kept where they are subjected to a sudden or severe drop in temperature, especially if the temperature change is linked to fewer hours of daylight. In general, hibernation is undesirable, for the hamster may not have sufficient stores of body fat to survive, and a sudden awakening can be dangerous.

Syrian Hamster To avoid the ambiguity of referring to a 'cream Golden Hamster', it is becoming increasingly popular to call *Mesocricetus auratus* the 'Syrian Hamster', following the practice of using geographical names for the other best-known species: the European, Russian and Chinese. The Golden Hamster is not exclusive to Syria, but it is indigenous there and has very strong connections with that country. In 1839 it was first collected and classified by Waterhouse on an expedition to the Syrian town of Aleppo. Almost a century later, when the species was thought to be extinct, another expedition discovered a female with her seven young and took them back to the Hebrew University at Jerusalem. Only three survived captivity but they bred with such success that it was claimed that the entire stock of laboratory and pet specimens was directly descended from the original trio of one male and two female hamsters.

Feet and claws The hamster sits up on its hind limbs when feeding and holds food in the forefeet. The forefeet are also used for pouching and de-pouching food. Claws tend to become overgrown in captivity, and may need occasional clipping.

Choosing a hamster

▶ A hamster can be very amusing to watch while it speedily and efficiently pouches its food, although most feeding takes place at night when hamsters are at their most active.

Which hamster?

The popular Syrian is one of the few small pets that must be kept singly, as two or more kept together will usually fight fiercely. Occasionally two of the same sex and from the same litter have been recorded living happily together, but they may turn on each other at any time.

There is one exception: occasionally golden hamsters have been kept successfully in a colony, but only in a very large compound with a series of individual nest areas. It has been found that, given enough space, Golden Hamsters will accept community living and communal areas provided that each animal has the exclusive use of a separate nest area and an approach ramp – which is defended jealously.

It is necessary to stress that these successful attempts at the colony rearing of adult Golden Hamsters have taken place either in schools or colleges where there are the facilities and space available to erect a really large compound. It is unlikely that you could supply suitable accommodation for a colony of hamsters under normal domestic conditions. If you wish to keep more than one hamster, you should find a supplier of the little Chinese or Russian (also known as Dwarf Russian) species (see pages 9 and 10). The Russians, in particular, are able to live together peaceably, but, in most respects, the care and requirements of these newcomers is the same as for the Syrian.

Guidelines to buying a hamster

Buying a hamster as a family pet, especially for a child, should always be a carefully considered decision, and the following points should be noted before rushing out to get one of these little animals.

Nocturnal lifestyle

Hamsters are normally awake from dusk, through the night, to dawn. They sleep during the day, which is very convenient if the family are out then, but the noise of an exercise wheel can be surprisingly loud and unrelenting at night. Although they are usually considered to be a children's pet, hamsters are not always awake when children are. However, by routinely offering its meal in the mid-afternoon, a young hamster can be acclimatized to rising a little earlier, but the animal should not be woken during the main period of its daytime sleep.

Age

It is best to acquire a young hamster so that it will soon enjoy being handled and become a good companion. Hamsters have quite a short lifespan (see page 46), so the younger the animal is, the better. Five to eight weeks is the age generally recommended. At this age, it will probably be nervous. To choose a good pet from a cageful of young hamsters, ignore any cowering in a corner or charging about panic-stricken. The most curious hamster should prove the most tamable.

Health

A healthy hamster should be plump, with soft, glossy fur over a clean skin, which is free of abscesses, sores or pimples, and especially of any dampness under the tail (see also page 39).

Sex

Unless the animal is required specifically for breeding, the hamster's sex is not important, although some people do prefer the female's more rounded shape, while others swear that the male lives a little longer. However, if a particular sex is wanted to complete a breeding pair, it is not unknown for pet shop assistants to make mistakes, so check for yourself whether it is a male or a female. The gap between the anus and the genital opening is much shorter in the female than the male.

▶ Healthy hamsters should be bright-eyed with soft, glossy fur and clean skin like this Variegated Piebald Syrian Hamster.

◀ This appealing little hamster is a blonde longhaired variety. You should be aware that longhaired hamsters will need some grooming.

Variety and colour
The colour of a hamster's fur is purely a matter of taste – among the Syrians there are over 100 combinations. However, do not opt for the longhaired variety unless you have both the time and the inclination to groom it at least every other day (see page 32).

Sources
The best place to buy a hamster for either breeding or showing is from a breeder who exhibits regularly at shows. You should seek out the secretary of your local hamster club who should be able to recommend a suitable breeder. However, many perfectly adequate pet hamsters can be acquired from pet shops or from a friend or acquaintance who is glad to find good homes for surplus youngsters.

Bringing your hamster home
You should prepare for your hamster's arrival and have a suitable cage ready before you acquire your new pet and bring it home. This should be warm (hamsters should be kept at a temperature that is no lower than about 18°C (65°F) or they may become dormant) and secure as hamsters are great escape artists (see page 19).

Your new hamster should be carried home in a small ventilated box or tin, with some hay or paper shavings inside for comfort. Allow it to run from this container into its cage, give it food and water (see page 26), and then leave it entirely alone for 24 hours to settle down. The temptation to peep at it or handle it should be strongly resisted.

Caging

Choosing a suitable cage

Since an adult Golden Hamster is likely to spend its entire life alone in captivity, the owner has a particularly strong responsibility to provide as large and as interesting an environment as possible for their pet. Enough is known about the habits of this hamster in the wild to judge accurately what kind of accommodation is required if the animal's needs are to be met in captivity. You must start with the cage.

▶ This style of cage with horizontal bars will allow your hamster to climb around its home. Check the strength of the clips holding the base in place.

◀ Tubular housing systems are suitable for smaller Chinese hamsters which will escape through the wires of other cages. Generally, you buy a starter kit and then add new sections to it, but cleaning this style of accommodation is often more difficult than a cage.

Being an underground creature by nature, possessing both strong nest-building and hoarding instincts, it is vital that the hamster should have some privacy and also the opportunity to burrow right out of sight when it chooses. Plenty of suitable bedding and burrowing materials are essential, together with a secluded place for sleeping and hoarding food. Apart from the size of the cage, privacy and the opportunity to burrow are the main requirements of the substitute environment that you create for your pet. Any hamster that is deprived of these comforts would be subjected to an unwarranted amount of stress.

Size

The size of cage is obviously important and, in this respect, a home-made cage may score over a commercially-produced one. However, size alone (see page 20) is not a sufficient guide to the suitability or otherwise of a particular cage. Golden Hamsters are very active, and the whole cage interior needs to be accessible if the animal is to enjoy the high level of activity that is natural to it.

Security

Security is a very important consideration. Apart from being highly active and agile, hamsters are also extremely competent at gnawing and will escape from a flimsy or insecure cage. Home-made cages need to be stout enough to withstand their constant gnawing, and commercial cages must be securely fastened.

Home-made versus commercial

Home-made cages need not be difficult to construct as you will discover on the following page. However, commercial cages are often suitable provided that they are properly used and are furnished with sufficient burrowing and bedding materials, with a 'gallery' level added if necessary. For most people, it is easier to visit their local pet store and buy a ready-made cage rather than make one themselves, but make sure that exercise wheels are fastened to the cage rather than being free standing, and are plastic with filled-in rungs.

▲ This larger enclosure will give a hamster plenty of space. As well as climbing, your pet could explore the tunnels and exercise on the wheel. The base can be easily detached for cleaning purposes.

The home-made enclosure

Size
Make the dimensions as generous as possible. Overall measurements of at least 75 x 40 x 40 cm (30 x 15 x 15 in) are recommended.

Wire mesh
A home-made enclosure should have a wire mesh insert for ventilation which can also serve as a climbing frame. The wire mesh should be securely fixed within a wooden surround. A hamster will gnaw away at a weak joint and will eventually escape.

▼ Floor space is important for hamsters. They must be able to move around, have somewhere to sleep and also possibly a wheel which will allow them to exercise.

Glass top
The enclosure can be fitted with a sliding glass top to allow good observation and access to the hamster with the minimum disturbance. The glass needs to slide on runners holding it securely in position. If the glass can be lifted at a corner, the hamster will soon escape.

Natural vegetable fibre

Soft paper bedding

Soft paper bedding

Construction

Hardwood is the best construction material when building a hamster enclosure, but soft wood with a smooth, laminated plastic finish (such as Formica) is a cheaper and more readily available alternative. The framework of the enclosure will be damaged by gnawing if it is left exposed.

Positioning the cage

Do not put your hamster's cage in direct sunlight as it will get hot very quickly. Also, you must ensure that the cage is kept well away from draughts.

Floor litter

The cage should be designed to make it possible to provide the hamster with a deep layer of suitable materials for shredding and burrowing. Always put a layer of coarse sawdust, which has absorbent qualities, on the base of the cage. Now add some layers of materials, such as medicated parchment, kitchen paper, hay and cardboard. Newsprint and magazines should not be used as the inks can be poisonous to hamsters. Cotton wool should not be used either. Leave the hamster to shred and arrange the materials as it wants.

▲ A wooden log will serve both as a toy and something your hamster can safely gnaw.

Drinking water bottle

A drip-feed water bottle should be suspended in the hamster's cage or enclosure. Keep the spout clear of the burrowing litter or water will leak from the bottle and make the whole cage damp.

Gnawing block

All hamsters need to gnaw, in order to wear down their long incisor teeth. If their accommodation provides them with plenty of material for shredding, the teeth are unlikely to become seriously overgrown. However, you should provide a hardwood gnawing block and some unshelled brazil nuts, dog biscuits or a carrot.

Gallery

A raised gallery extends the floor area and allows you easy access to the food containers. It lifts the exercise wheel and water bottle clear of the burrowing matter.

Food store

If the hamster is given such perishable foods as egg, cheese and fish, you must inspect the food store once every day or two. Hamsters are quickly upset if their hoard is disturbed, but it is equally important to remove discreetly any decaying food while the hamster is at play elsewhere.

Nesting box

Golden hamsters have a very strong nesting instinct. Provide a nest box, together with soft hay or bedding. Avoid using synthetic fibres, or any natural fibres such as knitting wools, which may cause obstruction if ingested. Occasionally, the hamster will move its nest. This is usually a temporary move, however, and the nest box should remain in place.

▲ Nests of this type are just one of the many options available for a hamster's sleeping quarters, which are available from pet stores.

▶ Hamsters are naturally inquisitive and always like to investigate all the objects in their quarters, even if they decide not to sleep in them.

Exercising

The need for exercise

Hamsters need to travel long distances in the wild, in order to collect enough food to survive in desert conditions. In captivity the opportunity to move around is largely removed, together with the urgent need to do so. Yet hamsters will still travel long distances every night on an exercise wheel because their instinct to be active remains. It has been demonstrated that caged hamsters thrive most when they are given plenty of opportunity for exercise, and the best accommodation should be designed with this need in mind.

◀ Household items, such as cardboard tubes from paper towels, are also appreciated by hamsters.

Enabling the hamster to use all the cubic space available in its accommodation is as important as the overall size. This is why devices such as ramps and galleries, bars for climbing, tunnels, a wheel and plenty of materials for gnawing, shredding and tunnelling should be included in its cage or enclosure. These have the effect of extending the confines of the cage and warding off boredom by providing the opportunity for a captive animal to keep itself well-occupied.

Exercise wheel

A solid wheel is preferable to one with open rungs, and it should be fixed close enough to the cage wall to prevent the hamster becoming trapped behind it. There has always been some controversy about the use of exercise wheels for pet rodents, because there are occasional reports of mishaps when animals become trapped in or behind the wheel, usually by a limb or the tail. The hamster, with its almost non-existent tail, is less at risk than some other rodents in this respect, and its great need for activity is usually considered to outweigh any slight risk of accident that may be present.

Care should always be taken if a female and her young are using a wheel together. The young tend to hurl themselves on the wheel – and on each other – and with each one pulling in a different direction there may be an increased risk of an accident and injuries.

The need for supervision

Captive hamsters seem to enjoy having a free play-time each day. Some owners give them a bucket of soil to dig in, or allow them the freedom of a room. Like all animals, hamsters vary in temperament. Some will lurk in the shadows behind the sofa whereas others will make straight for the curtains or the stair carpet – both of which they are able to climb. Some supervision is therefore essential!

Lost hamsters

There are, of course, hazards to such a free regime. Hamsters are notoriously quick and agile and frequently become lost. In one school, the hamster disappeared for three months and was found nesting in the dustbag of the vacuum cleaner. Another was lost on moving day but emerged later in the new house from a large potted plant!

Sometimes it is possible to recapture a lost hamster using a bucket or similar large container, made comfortable with a soft ball of bedding material, and baited with its favourite food. Use some books to create 'stairs' leading up to the top of the bucket and, hopefully, when the hamster sees the food it will tumble in and will be unable to escape. It is important to check the bucket regularly.

Feeding

In the wild, the Golden Hamster is thought to be mainly herbivorous, living on a diet of dry, wind-blown seeds, supplemented with occasional greenstuff, and possibly some small grubs and insects. In captivity, your hamster will thrive best on a diet of mixed seeds, grains and nuts. These may, if convenient, be bought in packets and can be supplemented with other cereal foods: wholemeal bread, puppy meal and porridge oats. Hamsters delight in extracting and pouching tiny fragments of kernel from piles of nutshells after the main part of the nut has been eaten.

Fresh food

Hamsters will eat many kinds of fresh fruit and vegetables, including apple, pear, tomato, salad greenstuff, cabbage, carrot, swede and wild plants, such as well-washed clover, dandelion and groundsel. Avoid plants from roadside verges or from any areas that may have been sprayed with chemicals. The following are poisonous to hamsters: coltsfoot, rhubarb leaves, potato tops and tomato leaves. Some animal protein may be occasionally introduced – sliced hard-boiled egg, pieces of cheese, flakes of cooked fish and small shreds of cooked meat.

How much and how often?

It is really only necessary to feed a hamster once a day. The main meal may be offered in the early evening, and later on (or in the morning) offer some greens, fruit and hard, chewy foods. As the hamster is a hoarding animal by nature, most food will be pouched and taken to the food store to be eaten later. Dry foods should be left undisturbed in the store, but any perishable foods should be removed, unobtrusively if possible, before they have time to rot.

◀ Seeds feature prominently in the diet of hamsters. They can use their front feet like hands to hold their food.

◀ Hamsters rely on their sharp incisor teeth to nibble off pieces of food which they can then stuff into their pouches. They seem to know almost instinctively just how large the pieces are that they can swallow.

A hamster's food intake is very small and if perishable food is regularly found hoarded, its rations are probably over-generous.

Water

Fresh drinking water must always be available. Since an open dish would soon be spilled or filled with cage litter, a drip-feed bottle is recommended. Check that the valve operates freely, and that the

▶ Hamsters enjoy a varied diet, the bulk of it being different types of seeds and nuts, much as it would be in the wild.

hamster does not pile up litter beneath the spout to make the bottle leak. To prevent algae, the water bottle can be painted black, but with the bottom left unpainted to check the water level.

There is no excuse for denying a hamster access to drinking water on the grounds that it is a desert animal. Conditions in the desert are harsh, but the hamster is free there and well adapted to survive by keeping below ground during the day. In its complex of underground burrows temperatures are equable, much lower than on the surface, and humidity is relatively high. The hamster also has the advantage of the morning dew, and is free to go off in search of green food, such as desert succulents, with their high water content.

By contrast, conditions in a cage would soon become intolerable unless you understand that, once restricted in captivity, your hamster is dependent on your help to provide sufficient water for its well-being.

▶ A hamster food mix may contain over a dozen ingredients.

Suggested diet chart

	What?	When?	How much?
Adult hamster	Mixed seeds, grains, nuts or hamster pellets, wholemeal bread, puppy meal and/or uncooked porridge oats	Early evening	About 1 heaped teaspoonful, but you can offer more for pouching and storing
	Fresh fruit and vegetables, and greenstuff which is well washed in cold water	Late evening or morning	As much as your hamster will consume in the same day
	Protein, such as chopped hard-boiled egg, cheese, scraps of fish, cooked meat	With either of above meals	Offer in very small amounts – no more than will be consumed in the same day
	Fresh water	Always available	
	Milk (preferably slightly sour)	Liked by many hamsters as part of routine diet, but should always be given if dietary deficiency is suspected	
Pregnant and lactating females	As above, but give milk routinely, plus mash of fine oatmeal or baby food with milk. Increase quantities, especially of the protein sources, as her appetite increases.		
Growing young	See page 43		

Handling

Children are sometimes disappointed to find that a newly acquired pet hamster is difficult to catch and may even bite. You need to explain to them that an animal which has been bred by a commercial breeder will have been handled very little prior to being sold. The hamster must be tamed before anyone can handle it confidently and easily.

Taming a hamster

This involves accustoming the hamster to being handled, and is usually achieved in the space of a few weeks. It takes patience, understanding and a little time. Young hamsters are easily tamed and may be touched safely just before weaning when they emerge from the nest to take solid food. By this time they are unlikely to be attacked by an over-anxious mother. Older hamsters can also be encouraged by gentle treatment to become tractable and friendly. Food is the way to any animal's heart, but don't point a finger at a hamster to sniff as it may mistake it for food and bite!

▶ Never hold a hamster tightly in your hand, as this is likely to cause it to bite you. This applies especially in the case of hamsters that are not accustomed to being handled regularly.

To entice a hamster from its nest, you should place some food in the cage and then tap gently on the cage side. The hamster will soon learn to associate the tapping sound with food.

Whatever the age of the animal, begin the taming process simply with stroking movements and hand-feeding during the active period. As soon as this is readily accepted without resentment or nervousness, begin lifting the animal by cupping it in your hands. Eventually progress to lifting the hamster by the loose skin at the back of the neck with your thumb and finger while supporting the body weight with your free hand at the same time. If you make a tunnel shape with each of your hands in turn, it will wriggle through from one hand to another.

Safety issues

Any hamster may make an unexpected jump if startled, so always handle it over a surface such as a table top for safety. Never let the hamster fall more than 20 cm (8 in) as serious injury is likely. If it is surprised by a sudden movement from above, the hamster is likely to freeze and then creep towards cover with its body flattened close to the ground. If the hamster is not used to exercising out of its cage, it is likely to be ill at ease in an exposed situation and may make a sudden dart for the cover of the nearest shadow. You should never disturb a sleeping hamster. However, a hamster that has been resting all day in a quiet house may rouse itself in response to the sound of the family returning home.

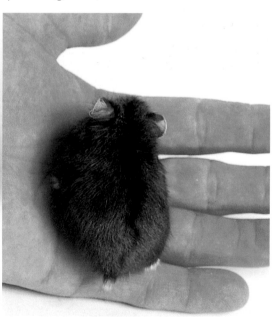

▲ Scent is very important in a hamster's life, because the eyesight of these rodents is relatively poor. Always allow your hamster to sniff your hand; it will soon realize that it has nothing to fear and then you can encourage it to step on to your hand.

Grooming and hygiene

Shorthaired varieties

A shorthaired hamster normally grooms itself very thoroughly, and only in exceptional circumstances would it need any assistance from you, the owner. Just occasionally a hamster may get unusually dirty – after an escapade up a chimney or in a coal cellar, for example. It would then probably need swabbing gently with a pad of cotton wool wrung out in warm water. Take veterinary advice about using detergent or any other substance on a hamster's fur contaminated by oil, for instance. (It is advisable not to allow free play in a garage or similar work area.)

Longhaired varieties

These hamsters should be groomed regularly – not only when the coat becomes matted, tangled and dirty. Grooming every other day is recommended to keep your pet's coat in good order. Use a soft dry toothbrush, dampened with some warm water if necessary, to restore a neglected or badly soiled coat to its proper condition.

Grooming as a displacement activity

When an animal is put into a difficult situation, it will often indulge in an irrelevant, completely disconnected activity that can do nothing to solve the problem, yet seems to relieve the feeling of stress. Biologists call this 'displacement activity', and a human parallel would be a worried person scratching his head or smoothing his hair.

▶ Longhaired hamsters will benefit from being groomed with a soft toothbrush. This provides a good opportunity to check the animal's coat, but always brush away from the head in order to avoid the hamster's prominent eyes.

You may notice that your pet may also use grooming movements as a displacement activity, indulging in unnecessary bouts of grooming when put into a stressful situation, such as a new environment, a freshly cleaned cage, or in the event of a confrontation with another hamster.

Teeth cleaning

The hamster's teeth can only be cleaned by working them on hard food, such as raw apple or carrot, and by gnawing on wood. You must provide hardwoods only, because hamsters may pouch splinters of softwood and damage the delicate pouch linings.

Cage hygiene

Traditionally designed cages need thorough cleaning once a week, whereas an enclosure will need cleaning and refurbishing about every two weeks. The hamster should meanwhile be lodged in a secure, ventilated box for safe keeping.

Each day, remove droppings, refill the water bottle, and extract greens and other perishable foods from the cage or, if need be, from the food store. If the bedding is clean, shake and replace it, adding a little more hay. Some hamsters are much more tidy than others, selecting different parts of their accommodation for urinating, defecating, and so on, which makes tidying the cage daily an easier and more effective task.

To avoid making the cage unduly damp, a young or newly acquired hamster can be trained to use a selected 'damp corner'. Any small, rigid plastic tray of sawdust will serve. Alternatively, a jam jar turned on its side or a corner cut from a firm plastic container can be used. If a little damp sawdust is retained and replaced each time the cage is cleaned, the hamster should soon learn by smell to urinate in the same place.

The healthy hamster

Hamsters are basically very healthy little animals if they are kept in good conditions and fed properly, but prevention of disease is better than cure. It is, therefore, important to look at and handle the hamster every day, in order to become familiar with the animal's appearance when it is well. It should then be much easier to spot any change for the worse. The main external signs of a healthy hamster are listed opposite.

▶ When they do fall ill, hamsters need prompt veterinary attention, in common with all the small mammals which have very poor powers of recuperation.

Signs of health

Anus	This should be clean, wth no staining, scouring or discharge.
Appetite	Good; should eat well during the active period and hoard food.
Breathing	Should be silent and regular.
Body	Should be well-fleshed and rounded; no growths, sores or swellings.
Claws	These should be short and trim; there should be no splits.
Coat	Should be clean and dry; no soiling, tangling or matting; no parasites.
Demeanour	Should be calm, quiet and restful during the day; highly active, quick, alert and agile in the active period.
Ears	Fur-covered when young, balding with age; not torn, no discharge.
Eyes	Should be bright and clear; no cloudiness, discharge or encrustation.
Feet	Strong and well-formed; no deformity, and weight distributed evenly.
Mouth	This should be clean; no sores or dribbling.
Movement	Quick, darting movement from exposed situations into shadow; good climbing and burrowing abilities.
Nose	This should be clear of any discharge or dried mucus.
Pouches	These should be used frequently, filled and emptied with the forefeet; no soreness or abnormal swelling.
Teeth	Should be clean and undamaged; front incisors worn down naturally on hard food and gnawing blocks.

Overgrown teeth

Without enough suitable gnawing material, the incisors can become so overgrown that the hamster cannot feed properly. Veterinary help is needed to correct this, after which a proper diet (see page 26) must be fed so the problem does not recur. If the hamster loses one tooth, its opposite number in the other jaw will grow too long and will need frequent cutting.

Overgrown claws

This usually happens with elderly hamsters. You can trim the claws very carefully with sharp scissors or animal nail clippers, but the claws must be held to the light to ensure no blood and nerve vessels are severed. It is safest to take a dark-coloured hamster to the vet for this procedure.

Keeping hamsters healthy

Hamsters normally remain free from disease and parasites if they are kept in good conditions and fed a suitable diet. It is important that they are not subjected to any unnecessary stress by having their mainly nocturnal routine disturbed unduly, as they do need quiet and privacy during the morning and early afternoon.

When you are away

Because hamsters store their food, it is possible for you to leave them unattended for a very short time, such as a weekend. This is totally contrary to the requirements of other mammalian pets, but hamsters will ration their food instead of gorging on it all at once.

Naturally, adequate water must be left for the whole period that you will be away, and the food should not include more perishable foodstuffs than the hamster will eat up completely on the first day of your absence. Any food it stores will then be non-perishable.

Ideally someone should come in to feed the hamster, as of course must happen if your absence is for a longer period. Leave a note of the hamster's food, water and bedding requirements, together with the vet's telephone number. Keeping the supplies near the cage is helpful. If your absence is for any length of time, the friend or neighbour will have to be prepared to clean out the cage and should be warned how to do this without losing the little animal. If the time span is short enough, only the damp corner should be cleaned, and the carer advised to leave the hamster in its cage. It is, of course, also possible to board hamsters with a vet or pet shop, or possibly a breeder.

▶ These young banded hamsters look fit and healthy. You should check your pet regularly for any signs of poor health.

First aid

In an emergency, you should always seek expert veterinary advice immediately. Pick up the hamster carefully and take it to your vet in a small secure container which is lined with hay. If you are not certain of the surgery hours, telephone first to make sure that the veterinary surgeon will be there to see your pet.

Falls
Probably the most frequent emergency problem with hamsters is that of a fall. Hamsters have a very delicate bone structure and are short-sighted, so they are prone to accidents. If the hamster seems distressed after a fall, it should be returned gently to its nest and then left alone to recover from the shock. If it does not seem to have recovered in an hour, or if broken bones or internal injuries are suspected, it should be taken immediately to your veterinary surgeon.

Hibernation
This is not an emergency, but it is recommended that a hamster found curled up in a hard ball, with shallow breathing (so that it may at first be mistaken for dead) should be revived slowly in your hands, or in a warm room. Hibernation can occur if the temperature in which the cage is kept is too low or drops suddenly.

Overheating
Caged animals like hamsters should never be left in direct sunlight. At temperatures above 27°C (80°F), hamsters can become rigid and apparently dead for several minutes. They may also quiver and shake. It may take a few minutes before the animal reverts to normal.

Wounds
Small clean wounds will usually heal themselves. Larger ones can be bathed in mild antiseptic, but a vet's advice is preferable, because of the risk of infection and of the abscesses that occur if the upper part of a deep wound heals over and traps dirt or bacteria inside.

Ailments

Abscesses and ulcers

These usually develop on a wound which has been caused by one hamster fighting another. If there is a discharge, bathe it with a mild antiseptic solution. Abscesses in the cheek pouches are more serious, and veterinary help should be sought in dealing with any abscess or ulcer that makes an animal unwell or is slow to heal.

Congenital defects

Certain defects, such as club foot and eyelessness, may be passed on genetically. Inexperienced breeders should understand that such animals must never be used for breeding, and that those suffering from a disabling defect should be destroyed humanely.

Impaction of pouches

Sometimes a hamster will pouch unsuitable materials which cause the cheek pouches to become impacted. Do not delay in asking your veterinary surgeon to remove the obstruction.

Inflammation or encrustation of the eyes

▼ Excessive grooming can be an indication of a skin irritation which is caused by parasites.

Conjunctivitis is a common complaint. It may be associated with upper respiratory tract infections or may be caused by an irritant such as sand, grit or dust. You should consult your veterinary surgeon in the early stages of the complaint. However, it may be that a hamster that fails to remove an encrustation around the eyes is suffering another sign of ageing. In this case, help the animal to groom properly by bathing around the eye with cotton wool wrung out in warm water.

Fur loss and sore skin

Although few hamsters live more than three years, they show definite signs of ageing. Loss of fur is nearly always such a sign. The ears go bald first, and then the body fur around the hindquarters and on the animal's underside. Sometimes the loss of fur is caused by friction, and it is usually accompanied by sores. It is necessary to remove the cause of friction, at least temporarily. Hair loss and irritation may also be associated with skin parasites such as mites, or, very occasionally, ringworm fungus. If in doubt, you should seek veterinary advice.

Poisoning by aerosols

Since hamsters spend so much time grooming, they are particularly at risk if poisonous aerosol sprays are used in the same room. Check the manufacturer's instructions concerning pets in the room before using a spray, or temporarily remove the hamster's accommodation until any airborne residue has settled.

▲ Constipation is more likely to arise in obese hamsters with a poor diet which is comprised mainly of sunflower seeds.

Respiratory disorders

Upper respiratory infections (colds) can occur, causing sneezing and catarrh, with a sore nose and eyes. It is believed that hamsters may be susceptible to human cold and influenza viruses. Pneumonia, with laboured breathing, can develop as a serious complication. Damp or draughty living conditions and poor nutrition encourage respiratory infection. Good nursing and a suitable environment are essential, and additional veterinary treatment may necessary.

Another cause of respiratory disorders in hamsters can be dusty, musty hay (or other bedding or burrowing materials) to which the animal may develop an allergic reaction.

Wet tail

This highly infectious disease of the bowel is thought to be associated with stress – a sudden change in the diet and/or environment. Wet tail quickly spreads and is dreaded by those who keep a large hamstery.

The non-specific early symptoms of wet tail, which you should look out for, are a general loss of coat condition, listlessness and a lack of interest in food. These are followed by characteristic watery diarrhoea from the anus. This makes the fur around the tail constantly wet and accounts for the name of the disease.

If you suspect that your hamster is suffering from wet tail, you must seek prompt veterinary attention, but even so this disease is often fatal. Strict hygiene is necessary, particularly if the cage or its accessories are to be re-used, or if more than one hamster is kept, even though they are in separate cages.

Reproduction

A female hamster will probably produce between five and seven young in a litter, and within two months of their birth each will need a separate cage! So it is essential to know that good homes can be found for them all before you even start to think of mating any of your hamsters. Since most owners only keep one hamster, the question of breeding does not normally arise, and certainly breeding by amateur keepers cannot be recommended. However, if you are seriously considering breeding, you should seek plenty of advice first, if possible from several experienced breeders.

Mating

Syrian Hamsters are difficult to pair up even for mating and, unless the conditions are right, the female hamster will turn on the male in a most aggressive fashion. She may even inflict serious injuries on him if they start to fight. A female will never allow a male into her own territory, and she is rarely receptive in his. The only way in which you can encourage them to mate is to introduce them to each other on some neutral ground – which is new to them both – and unless she shows

▼ A pregnant Chinese Hamster. Their gestation period is about 21 days, whereas that of the Dwarf Russian is usually around 18 days.

some sign of being receptive quickly, then you must be prepared to separate them again before any fighting can begin.

It is wise to supervise the pairing session wearing some stout gloves, so that the two hamsters can be parted by hand if necessary. When the female is receptive to the male, which will nearly always be in the evening during the natural period of activity, you can leave them together for about 20 minutes – this is quite sufficient. When the female is unreceptive, you should abandon the session and try the pairing again on several consecutive evenings, remembering that she comes into season every fourth day.

Pregnancy and birth

As a member of a solitary species, the female hamster will rear her young entirely alone, with no help from the male who must be taken from her immediately after copulation, and with no assistance from humans, whose interference she is likely to resent.

The female should be provided with plenty of extra bedding and nesting materials, such as soft hay, in her own accommodation. She will construct a nest which may be open-topped during a hot spell.

She also needs to be given plenty of fresh drinking water at all times since pregnant animals usually drink more than usual, and she will benefit from having some milk at this time. Her normal diet should be increased in amount and quality. In particular, increase the protein, including the animal protein, in her diet. She will need this extra nutrition during pregnancy and lactation.

Breeding puts a great strain on the female, both physically and mentally, since she has the entire responsibility for her litter, which may amount to a dozen or more and is invariably boisterous.

Breeding age

Although it is usual for males to become sexually capable of breeding during their sixth week, and females during their eighth week, breeding is best postponed until a minimum age of 12–14 weeks is reached. A professional breeder would expect a female to bear no more than three litters during her breeding life, which lasts until she is twelve months old. To prevent her becoming exhausted and bearing litters of poor quality, it is essential that she be rested between each family.

If, as is usual, the first litter is conceived when the female is about three months old, the second should not be conceived before the age of six months, and mating for the final litter should be delayed until the female reaches the age of nine months.

The young

Syrian Hamsters have the shortest gestation period of any mammal, lasting only 16 days. As a result of this brief pregnancy, the young are born very immature – they are blind, furless and completely helpless. By seven days, their fur has developed, although it is usually paler than it will be on the adult animal.

Litters tend to be in the range of five to seven young, but much bigger litters of 14–17 are not unknown. Most female hamsters of this species bear 14 nipples – an indication that large litters are usual. However, a litter of 14 young would weigh not more than 28 g (1 oz).

Experienced handlers will lure the female away from the young in order to inspect a young litter, but this is always chancy since newborn hamsters are at risk from attack by their own mother if she or they are disturbed. It is safer for a novice breeder to forgo observing the very early stages of development. The droppings tray should be cleaned out every day, but the nest should be left alone unless it absolutely has to be examined. Never use your fingers – instead, you can open the top of the nest slightly with a piece of wood rubbed in cage litter. The female should be removed first, and then distracted with food when she is returned to the cage.

▶ These Roborovski's Dwarf Hamsters are just six days old and they are developing rapidly. You must keep disturbances to a minimum while the young are still in the nest.

Growth and development

The female has to tend her litter entirely alone, since Syrian Hamsters are not family animals. Early growth is rapid, and the young may be expected to emerge from the nest during the second week of life, when they will begin to take solid food, such as fine oatmeal, puppy meal and finely chopped greenstuff. By three or four weeks, the young will have completed the transition to solid food. They are likely to be quite independent by the end of the fourth week, and sometimes earlier.

If the mother shows signs of being exhausted or exasperated, the young may be removed from her as soon as they have been weaned, and then live together in a colony for a further week or two.

At five to six weeks, as they begin to reach puberty, the rough and tumble play of the young will turn to real fighting, and they will be liable to mate each other. It is therefore essential that after this time each hamster should be housed individually.

The females tend to be noisier and more aggressively territorial than the males, but either sex is delightful. These solitary animals are more than usually dependent on their owners, but if your lone hamster is given good living conditions, the opportunity to exercise and plenty of attention, it will prove to be an engaging pet.

▲ This litter of young Syrian Hamsters are just over three weeks old. They are still with their Cinnamon mother.

Your questions answered

Is it all right to feed my hamster small sweets as an occasional treat?

Very definitely, no! Food that is foreign to any animal's diet can cause an upset stomach and, if fed in excessive quantities, death. In the wild, hamsters will feed mainly on seed, grain and, when they can find it, vegetable matter. In captivity their diet should reflect this – check the table on page 29 which lists a variety of suitable food. For a treat, try giving your hamster a grape, some sultanas, or perhaps a tiny chunk of hard cheese to gnaw on. Never be tempted to see whether it likes things like sweets and chocolate – even a small piece represents a large amount to such a tiny animal.

Whenever I try to pick up my hamster, it bites. Am I doing something wrong?

Probably the hamster is scared of you and trying to protect itself. If you are patient, you should be able to overcome this. Start by simply stroking the hamster and hand-feeding it when it is active. When it no longer seems to resent this or to be nervous, try lifting it by cupping it in your hand. Eventually you should be able to lift the hamster by the loose skin at the back of the neck, while supporting its body weight with your other hand.

Why does my hamster spend hours gnawing at his cage?

Basically, this is due to boredom. You should give your hamster plenty of opportunities for exercise and interesting things to do.

My neighbour's hamster recently died of hypothermia. What precautions should I take to avoid mine going the same way?

For a start, don't let the room that houses the hamster's cage become too cold; if there is any danger on a chilly night, then move the cage into a warmer area. If your precautions fail and the hamster appears dead, it may have gone into hibernation. You could try warming it up in the airing cupboard.

Can you train hamsters not to soil their bedding? Mine never seems to use the tray provided.

Some hamsters seem to be tidy, others not. Try cleaning out the cage very thoroughly, and put a small amount of soiled litter back in the area you want to be used as a toilet. With luck, the hamster will catch on. Alternatively, are you cleaning the cage out frequently enough? If it is smelly all over, the hamster is unlikely to distinguish between its bed and its lavatory.

How can I make a room hamster-proof? I like to let mine out to run around, but she always manages to escape.

There's no magic formula, except to say that hamsters can find their way into very tiny gaps, and can also climb and jump higher than you would ever imagine. If, despite your best endeavours, your hamster keeps disappearing, try watching her like a hawk all the time she is out, to find out exactly where she goes. You may then discover her escape route. However, do not worry too much if she does disappear temporarily. She will usually return, especially if you put the open cage on the floor with some food inside.

When I clean out my hamster's cage, I'm always surprised to find how much food he has stored in his nesting box. Some of it is mouldy. Do you think I am feeding him too much?

Yes! You should cut down on the usual amount you feed him each day.

My granddaughter longs for a pet of her own. Would a hamster be a suitable Christmas present?

No pet, large or small, should ever be given as a surprise present, especially at Christmas. There is too much noise and excitement, and no time to introduce the animal quietly and carefully. The young animal may be nervous, pining for its mother and siblings, and what it needs is absolute peace and quiet – not a noisy family celebration. Also, Christmas is always a bad time to buy a hamster. Relatively few animals are born during the winter and those that are available in the pet shops may have been weaned too early, specifically to catch the Christmas trade. Finally, remember that a hamster is not necessarily an ideal pet for a small child, owing to its nocturnal habits (see page 14).

Life history

Scientific name	*Mesocricetus auratus*
Gestation period	16 days (average)
Litter size	5–7 (average)
Birth weight	2 g ($^1/_{14}$ oz) average weight
Eyes open	12 days (approx.)
Weaning age	21–27 days
Puberty	45–60 days
Adult weight	100 g ($3^1/_2$ oz) average weight
Best age to breed	12 plus weeks (see page 41)
Oestrus (or season)	Every four days
Duration of oestrus	4–23 hours (typically persists for an evening)
Retire from breeding	Males: 15 months Females: 12 months
Life expectancy	18 months–2 years average (males tend to outlive females)

Index

Why not learn more about other
popular pets with further titles from
the bestselling RSPCA Pet Guide series?

PET GUIDE

C Collins Care for your
Kitten
0-00-718271-6

C Collins Care for your
Puppy
0-00-718268-6

C Collins Care for your
Rabbit
0-00-718270-8

C Collins Care for your
Goldfish
0-00-718272-4

C Collins Care for your
Guinea Pig
0-00-718269-4

C Collins Care for your
Budgerigar
0-00-719358-0

C Collins Care for your
Cat
0-00-719356-4

Paperback
£4.99   48pp

C Collins Care for your
Hamster
0-00-719357-2

C Collins Care for your
Tropical Fish
0-00-719359-9

To order any of these titles, please telephone **0870 787 1732**
For further information about all Collins books, visit our website: **www.collins.co.uk**